KT-489-662

Learning Maps and Memory Skills

REVISED SECOND EDITION

Ingemar Svantesson

 KOGAN PAGE | *CREATING SUCCESS*

Acknowledgements

Many friends and colleagues have contributed to make this book possible. In particular, thank you to: Malcolm Dennis, Sarah Dinsdale, Niels Gottlieb, Åsa Lundqvist, Rosemary Palmer, Irene Pearson, Dougal and Louise Thompson, and Dr Ashley Wilson.

First published in Sweden by Seminarium; English language edition published by Swan Communications Limited, New Zealand in 1989

First published in Great Britain in 1990 by Kogan Page Limited
Reprinted 1991, 1992, 1994 (twice)

Second edition published in 1998
Revised edition 2004

Kogan Page Limited
120 Pentonville Road
London N1 9JN

British Library Cataloguing in Publication Data

A CIP record for this book is available from the British Library.

ISBN 0 7494 4128 3

Typeset by Saxon Graphics Ltd, Derby
Printed and bound in Great Britain by Clays Ltd, St Ives plc

contents

background

The purpose of this book is to present a step-by-step guide into the learning maps technique and how to make the most of your memory. It is the result of more than 1000 courses and seminars which I have conducted throughout Sweden, Norway, Finland, the Netherlands, the UK, Australia and New Zealand since 1983. It is also based on four previous books I have written on similar subjects in Swedish.

New aspects appear all the time and people come up with brilliant ideas in the seminars. When those ideas have been tested, they gradually slip into books and contribute to the development.

how to use this book

This is a 'how-to-do-it' book, which means you will find a lot of exercises in it. Take time to do them all. You can't learn a new technique just by reading *about* it, you have to practise!

Start by reading quickly or just looking through all the pages, which will give you an idea of what the book is about and how it is structured.

Before you start practising, get some A4 or A3 unruled paper. You also need five or six different coloured pens with thin tips and two or three highlighter pens.

To store the learning maps you can use ordinary binders or if you use a planner, fit the maps into the project or key area to which they belong.

what is a learning map?

Learning maps are a *note-taking technique*. This technique could be used in a number of situations:

- for **planning**: personal planning, projects, sales, or any kind of planning where you need an overview
- for **problem solving**
- when you make **summaries**, eg of a book, a lecture, a radio or TV programme
- when you need a **structure**
- for **brainstorming** and **idea generation**
- for **note taking:** meetings, lectures, debates, interviews, etc and many more. You will find a lot of ideas and examples in this book.

... and why should you use it?

When you start using learning maps you will immediately notice several positive effects:

- If you find it difficult to memorize what you have written down, eg during a meeting or lecture, you will soon notice that your maps **improve your memory**.
- Note taking in the traditional, linear way takes too much time, as most people write down too many words. Using learning maps instead, you realize that this technique **saves time**. You don't need a lot of words to remember. As a result of using fewer words, you will find you can spend more time listening, taking part in discussions, etc. And as it saves time you will **get more things done!**
- Many people have difficulties putting things in the right place, in order to find them again when they need them. This also goes for note taking. As learning maps save time and space, you could easily find what you are looking for.

Using learning maps is an effective means of **getting organized!**

- At first glance a map may seem disorderly or even totally incomprehensible (see figure over the page). However, when you have made your maps you will notice that a learning map is generally more **structured and logically built up** than linear notes. This also helps you to find what you are looking for.
- You will make use of your **creative thinking** and **imagination** in many ways.
- Using learning maps is fun! Note taking is considered a tiring preoccupation – learning maps are not!

These are just a few of the effects and benefits from using learning maps as your note-taking system. You will find more while you are practising.

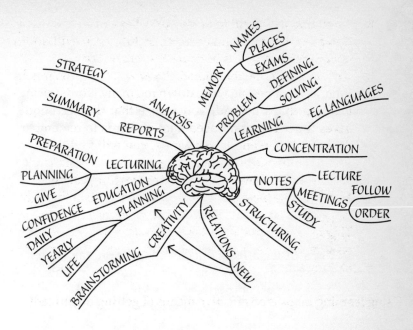

getting started

Learning maps differ a lot from 'ordinary' note-taking techniques. Most people take notes in full sentences or fragments of sentences. A smaller proportion use keywords only. Have a look at the map on page 99. How does this differ from your ordinary notes? Does it look messy? In a way it does, as you probably don't understand what the words and the pictures all mean – and where do you start reading? You may even think this is not worth trying to understand. However, it will all become clear once you get started.

In this chapter you will learn the first, elementary rules of learning maps step by step. You will not find it difficult if you follow the book through, do all the exercises and practise whenever you have a chance.

If you do that you will very soon get used to the technique and see the possibilities in it. What seems messy in a learning map when you first see one will soon appear to be very strict logic and you will easily find your way through it. However, if you are not used to taking notes at all, you may first have to practise picking out the right words. You may have to train your ability to listen, to find a context or a vital thought in what is being said or in what you are reading. These are skills you will practise in the first exercises.

Don't expect everything to come at once. Some people know how to ride a bike the first time they try, while others have to practise and practise. As with many other techniques, you will find that progress is made gradually or comes in leaps.

When schoolchildren learn how to read, some of them are so focused on the technique itself, they do not have the faintest idea what they have just been reading. But after a while when they have practised the skills, they also understand what they are reading and enjoy it.

When you master a technique and are then asked to learn one more or to replace the old one with a new, you will find yourself in conflict. Normally, you first get confused and try to apply the old rules to the new one. You get a mixture of both. To some people this is as far as they can get. They never really learn the new techniques or methods, because they don't see how they can do it.

To others, a new way of looking at things is an exciting challenge. So persevere, and when it all comes clear to you it will be very satisfying.

'ordinary' note taking

too much and no system

A lot of people are dissatisfied with their note taking. They realize that they take down too many words, which in turn makes it difficult to get an overview. They find it difficult to sort the essential facts from a lecture, a meeting or a book. Very few have had a satisfactory training in effective study skills and note taking.

Let's follow a student who has just arrived in the first term at university.

The professor drew down his specs and raised his hand with a reserved movement. It was the gesture of a conductor assembling the orchestra. Forty-two pencils were lifted over 42 note pads. He started to talk and everyone folded over their note pads and wrote as quickly as they could.

No one could take down in shorthand but they all tried their best to do some speedwriting. Forty-one male students and one female tried to take down as many notes as they could of what one of the foremost orators of their age was saying.

They wrote as many words as they could, but it was not nearly enough. The words were chasing each other, the students were left behind and had to take a jump every now and then to catch up. To understand the meaning of what they heard and to write it down at the same time, was simply impossible, nothing stayed, it was like raking long straw lengthways. They did not know what they wrote and when they saw what they had written down, they got startled and changed their tactics. They started to listen more coherently and took down brief summaries. But while they were writing, the lecture went on and when they were ready to listen again, the thread was broken and the next summary was hanging on its own. However they tried it, it was a patched job.

An author who had just learned how to use learning maps put a flip chart in his study. When he was working on a new book he started by making a draft of the whole book. Then he tore down that sheet and put it up somewhere else in the room. After that he made a new draft of each chapter.

Before he started to use learning maps he had had all these thoughts and ideas in his head, unstructured and unfinished. The writing process was associated with a lot of pain and negative feelings, for the author as well as for people around him.

By using learning maps he could now write down ideas and sudden flashes, without having to think of where to put them. It was always possible to change and restructure at any stage of the process. When he began writing he could do it without feeling any pressure or stress. He also noticed that he gained a lot of time as everything was so well structured and thought through when he started.

Another man, a scientist, who now and then gave open lectures to various groups of people, normally wrote down his full manuscript – every sentence of it! During the lectures he would read the manuscript word by word to the audience. He was not pleased with this procedure, as he thought his lectures were a bit 'dry' and impersonal (which his audiences would agree with!).

When he learned to use learning maps he started by making a rough draft in the form of a mind map. He tried to put himself in the place of the listener: 'What do I want to know about this subject?' By putting a number of such questions to himself he found more and more aspects of his subject.

One of the advantages of using learning maps is the ability to jump from one part of it to another, giving your thoughts a free flow.

The first time he tried the new technique he still wanted to write down his full manuscript in a linear form 'just in case', but he soon found that step unnecessary. So he started to use a learning map instead, redoing it to make it clearer, bigger and better structured, and he also used colours, symbols, pictures and three-dimensional illustrations. When he wanted to include facts in the form of graphs or charts he put them in the margin, or just kept them ready for quotation on another sheet of paper.

Both he and his audiences noticed the difference. His lectures became more vivid and interesting and he kept eye contact with the audience. All he had to do was to glance quickly at the learning map now and then to see if he had forgotten anything or to check what was next on the list.

These examples will do so far. What are your own motives for using learning maps, or rather – what motives do you have for *not* using maps?

Let this question stay in your head unanswered while you get more acquainted with the technique. When you learn and start practising learning maps you will discover the many advantages and areas of application.

Learning maps will help you to develop your creative as well as your analytical and logical abilities. You will learn how to find a structure and build connections between the various parts. It is important that you find your own personal style. No single learning map resembles another, even if two people make learning maps from the same meeting or text. The main thing is that your learning map can be used for the purpose you intended. It is always the result that counts.

keywords

The parts of speech all play their specific roles in language. Keywords are words you pick out of a text and store in your memory. They help you to recall the text when you need it.

Let's try an exercise:

exercise

In the following text we have removed all words but those that are **describing** something – how it looks, etc. What information do you get when you read these words? Every dash means a word has been omitted. Write down the associations you get from the words in the text.

— — — — — — — — — — — — — — . — — — — — —
— — — — — — . Casually — — — — , — — — — — — —
— — ornamental — — , — yellow — gaily marked, — — —
—, — — — alongside — — — perpendicularly. — — — —
— — — — — — , — — — — — — — — — — — , young —
attractive. — — — — — — — — — — — — — —, — — — — —
— — — — beneath — — .

Of course it is impossible to know exactly what this text is about by looking only at these words. But they do give you some information – they seem to describe a person and/or an object.

Let's add all the other words, except the verbs and the nouns, and see what happens:

The — he — in this — — to a — — — — . Through a — of this — — the — between — and — . Casually — over the — , — — — down the — before him an ornamental — — , — yellow and gaily marked, — by two — , a — — alongside — a — perpendicularly. The — — — with — — and — — , and on the — of the whole — a — , young and attractive. — — not — the — for more than half a — , when the — — — to a — just beneath his — .

Isn't it strange to discover how little some words mean? Let's add all the verbs as well and see what happens

The — he was in this — sloped to a — called — — . Through a — of this — ran the — between — and — . Casually glancing over the — , — saw coming down the — before him an ornamental — — , painted yellow and gaily marked, drawn by two — , a — walking alongside bearing a — perpendicularly. The — was laden with — — and — — , and on the — of the whole sat a — , young and attractive. — had not beheld the — for more than half a — , when the — was brought to a — just beneath his — .

There are 27 nouns in this text out of a total of 109 words. Still it is not clear what this text is about. Perhaps some of the verbs, such as *painted, drawn, walking, bearing, was laden* and *sat* will give you some clues?

Here are the missing words!

The **field** he was in this **morning** sloped to a **ridge** called **Norcombe Hill.** Through a **spur** of this **hill** ran the **highway** between **Emminster** and **Chalk-Newton**. Casually glancing over the **hedge, Oak** saw coming down the **incline** before him an ornamental **spring waggon**, painted yellow and gaily marked, drawn by two **horses**, a **waggoner** walking alongside bearing a **whip** perpendicularly. The **waggon** was laden with **household goods** and **window plants**, and on the **apex** of the whole sat a **woman**, young and attractive. **Gabriel** had not beheld the **sight** for more than half a **minute**, when the **vehicle** was brought to a **standstill** just beneath his **eyes**.

(From *Far from the Madding Crowd* by Thomas Hardy)

Well, were you able to guess the content of the text? Perhaps some of the small pieces of information you got from the start could have helped you in the right direction?

Let's do it the other way round. In the text below you have all the nouns. Try to find out what this text is about:

— — — people — — oceans, continents — rivers — — — United States. — — — — language — — — race, religion — nation — — world.

— — — newcomers — poverty — search — — — opportunities. — — — — — persecution — search — — freedom. — United States — — — symbol — democracy — freedom. — — — — — — — society — — — pot, — — — — — decades Americans — — — — — — — — — society — — — communities, — — — — — — — — — — — — .

— fact, — United States — — — — — — communities — — — — — — wealth. — reality — dreams — success — — — — — factors.

(From *Americans and the US* by Frederic Fleisher, Seminarium 1987)

Now, do you need the missing words? Probably not. You get enough information with the nouns to find a meaning in the text as it is.

in a nutshell

- ■ **Nouns** denote things, and they carry the information in a text.
- ■ **Verbs** denote activities, things that happen or what someone does.

■ **Adjectives** describe what things look like. They are linked to nouns and modify their meaning in describing or limiting them.

We mainly use these three parts of speech when we pick keywords, whatever note-taking technique we use, simply because they provide us with the information we need. The nouns are the most important ones. This does not mean you should exclude other words. **Keywords** are simply the words that **give you the best conclusions**.

the 'right' word

The ability to pick the right word or keyword is vital if you want to remember the most important information from any text.

Many students complain of having to spend so much time studying at home and yet, when they come to school or class the next day, it is all gone. Most of them lack the ability to pick out the right words as keywords and use them as 'hooks' for the rest of the information.

Generally, one could say that most people take too many notes and underline too many words in their books when they are studying. It may even be as much as 60 to 90 per cent too much. With so many words in the note pad, the revision of the material will also take a lot of time – and it is not even guaranteed you will understand what you have written down. When you revise things you have learnt, you only need a very limited number of words, **provided they are the right words!**

However many facts you present, however hard you study, however many beautiful and instructive pictures you have, what it all comes down to is how much you have learned from it and how much can you remember.

In the next exercise you have a longer text to read. Turn to page 15 and read Chapter 5, 'The Human Brain'. Underline and / or write down in you note pad the words you consider to be keywords.

levels in the language

By grouping the keywords into language levels you become more aware of what type of words you should concentrate on.

We can construct a 'language staircase', where we start from details in the language and step up to more general and over-lapping words. It is also a matter of stepping up from a concrete level of detail to an abstract level. Let's have a look at an example:

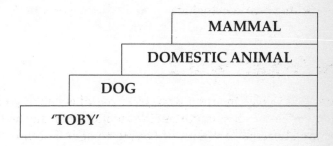

At the bottom of this generalized staircase you will find all the details in a text, in this case symbolized by the name of a dog. When it comes to talking about all the Tobys, Fidos, Spots and whatever the dogs are called, it is more practical to speak about them as 'dogs'. The next step puts the dogs into the same category as a group of other animals and the highest step on this staircase includes all animals of the category 'mammals'. On this step the dog is no longer visible, it has become a detail in a much larger context.

When you are making learning maps it is necessary to keep this classification in mind. The foremost task for keywords is to act as 'keys', just as the word suggests. They should unlock whole contexts, even years after you make your notes. They should give you the right associations directly – if you have chosen the right keywords!

Imagine a field of flower buds. With your video camera you take pictures of the buds – one picture every ten minutes until they open up into flowers. When you show the film the process will be much quicker than in reality. The image of these flower buds blooming may symbolize how the keywords work in your brain. A word that 'turns into a flower' is a word that will hold many associations. Some of these words will hold the content of a whole text, while others reveal smaller parts of the text.

Conversely, in the same way as the flower draws all the petals back to a bud again, a word may draw back its associations into its 'bud' and keep them locked up in the brain until you need them again. If it is a good keyword it will show all its 'petals' when it appears. New facts are hooked to the existing associations on various levels in the pattern. If they stay and could be retrieved we call it **learning.**

When you practise picking out keywords, you will probably find that you tend to take down too many words, 'just in case'. Try hard to reduce the number of keywords. It is a lot better to concentrate on finding keywords that function as flower buds.

This does not mean you should pick words mainly from the upper steps of the staircase where you find the abstract or general words. It might equally be concrete details that give you the best associations; sometimes it is an example or a story. In a learning map you use every level of language and also non-verbal information, such as pictures, colours, symbols, learning, etc.

the human brain

Before we go any further we shall look into some of the basics of how the human brain functions.

Your brain is made up of something like 10–1000 billion neurons or nerve cells. Most of these cells develop at an early stage in life.

Each of these cells is capable of developing thousands of synapses, which are the connections to other cells in the brain. The more of these synapses you have, the more connections you are able to make. The early experiences in your life determine how well those connections will function and how many you are able to make.

The organism with the highest number of connections produces the most complex, 'intelligent' behaviour. A low number of connections gives only a low number of possible reactions.

Those parts of the human body that perform the most complex movements demand a relatively higher portion of neurons in the brain. A hand, for example, is served by a larger number of neurons than a foot.

The human ability to speak is inherited, which is shown in the brain by the larger number of neurons that serve the mouth, the tongue and the larynx, compared with monkeys or other close relatives. The brain coordinates impulses from our senses to produce the appropriate behaviour.

The fact that the brain has two sides is not new, but the research that has been done mainly since the 1960s has led to some interesting discoveries.

The American Roger Sperry, who was later awarded the Nobel Prize in Medicine, led that research. He started a number of experiments on monkeys, which had their corpus callosum (the band of some 300 million nerve cell fibres connecting the two cerebral hemispheres) cut off. He found the monkeys could still behave in an apparently normal way and they could still learn new things. What he discovered was that the two hemispheres of the monkey brain seemed to live their own lives without knowing what the other half was doing.

Sperry then heard about similar operations on human beings with severe epilepsy. They also functioned in a normal way after the operation without any consequences on their memory learning abilities. In cooperation with these split-brain patients he then performed a number of interesting experiments.

It was already known that the ability to speak is a left hemisphere activity. Could the patients then talk about something that only the right hemisphere had 'seen'? As the left hemisphere directs the activities of the right half of the body and the right hemisphere directs the left half of the body, the experiments were arranged so that a picture could only be seen by one eye. When the patient was asked to tell what he had seen he could only name the pictures he had seen with his right eye. However, he could use his left hand to pick out the objects he had seen with his left eye.

The right hemisphere is 'mute', but is very skilled at distinguishing colours and forms. The right hemisphere also seems to be more skilled at distinguishing dimensions, patterns and wholeness, while the left hemisphere is more verbal and handles information in a sequential, logical way.

As a simplification, one could say that the left hemisphere can't see the forest because of the trees, while the right hemisphere can see the forest but not the trees. This means that each hemisphere is susceptible to different types of impulse. Logical, structured language is more suitable to the left hemisphere, while associations, pictures and analogies, the language of poetry and myths, is the kind of language that suits the right hemisphere. These two types of language also give different descriptions of reality, where intellect is opposed to intuition and feelings.

In western societies 'left-brain skills' are highly appreciated. During the last five to ten years we have become aware of the imbalance and its consequences. We have begun to value creativity in people more and to train people in whole-brain skills. We know from schools which put a lot of emphasis on art, music, literature and other creative skills that the students perform a lot better also in mathematics, languages and other 'left- brain skills'.

the unknown brain

We actually know very little about the way a brain functions. Most of what we do know has been 'discovered' in brain research during the last 10 to 15 years.

The information that comes in through our senses is filtered and compared with previous experiences. The impressions are being kneaded in mysterious ways, plastered and painted. Most of these impressions are well known to us in one form or another. Memory offers a fine scale map, where almost every piece of information will find its place – consciously or unconsciously.

When we come across something absolutely new, as with the picture on the next page, it will cause disruption in our brains. What is in this chaos of an apparently random pattern of black and white patches?

Your brain tries desperately to grasp the meaning of the pattern. Most people are unable to interpret the picture. Let me give you some clues: what is meant to be in the picture is a part of something that is real, a live being, very familiar to you. Now try again! Could it be a face? A woman? A dog? A horse? When you think you have discerned something meaningful in the pattern, have a look at page 104, where you will find a picture of what is in this pattern.

When you have seen the original, compare the two pictures. Can you see it now? How do you compare?

Most people look for outstanding features, things that are unique or typical. There is, of course, a reason for that. When you are in a complex situation, for instance in a traffic jam during rush hour, you have to interpret the elements in the right way in order to survive it.

where do ideas come from?

A very exciting new way of looking at brain functions has been presented by the Finnish brain researcher Matti Bergström, professor of neurophysiology at the University of Helsinki, Finland.

He was puzzled by the problem of how ideas are generated in our brains. Why isn't the 'output' the same as the 'input', or put another way, how can we generate completely new, even unexpected, thought patterns?

In his research Matti Bergström found that the brain could be described as a bi-polar system.

The brainstem is the oldest part of the brain. With its impulses it regulates our level of consciousness. The brainstem is one of the two poles.

The other pole is the cortex, the 3 mm folded layer of nerve cells, covering the two hemispheres. The cortex is divided into four lobes, involved in functions which include planning, receiving sensory information from the body, adjusting behaviour, making decisions, memory and perception.

These two poles generate impulses that influence the brain functions in two ways. The brainstem generates cascades of random signals – disorder, chaos. Matti Bergström names that part the 'chance generator'. The cortex is the 'knowledge generator'. It generates information – order.

He says:

When the random signals from the brainstem and the organized signals from the cortex meet, we get an interaction, a battle between chaos and order. On that 'battleground', in the perpetual battle between the two poles in your brain, there will be a lot of casualties. Complex patterns of information ('knowledge') will be bombarded by the chaotic impulses from the brainstem and be shattered. There will also occur 'mutations' in the thought patterns, ie totally new patterns, unexpected, unforeseeable ideas will be formed. In our everyday language we call them 'flashes' or 'bright ideas'.

Let me show you with a picture:

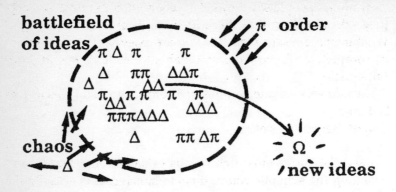

The knowledge formations, represented by a number of p, *meet cascades of impulses from the brainstem:* D. *In the battle between these two types of impulse, new forms are created:* Ω.

Matti Bergström says: 'It's here on the "battlefield of ideas" that we see the new forms appear, the phenomenon we call *creativity*.'

People who suffer from mental diseases can't cope with all these new ideas. They get hallucinations and agony from not being able to handle them with their knowledge. There are, of course, people with the opposite imbalance – people with such a strong 'knowledge generator' that they don't permit any new ideas at all! In the kind of societies we live in, where knowledge and facts are valued higher than imagination and creativity, we don't consider that imbalance to be a mental disease; those people are often chosen or elected to lead the rest!

Creativity is stimulated when we move the balance a little towards chaos and disorder. That is an explanation of why most people are creative when they have fun or are relaxed. The process goes on in the brain all the time, even when we are asleep, but the balance is then very near the impulses from the brainstem. That could be an explanation of why our dreams often are so fragmentary or even weird. We don't have access to the structured information from the cortex other than in fragments, coming up from the subconscious level.

Although people say they get excellent ideas while they sleep, they will also find that these ideas seldom survive daylight! What may seem sensible while you are asleep often turns out to be completely silly when you are able to evaluate it with your full senses.

How do we evaluate new ideas? There are good ones as well as bad ones.

Matti Bergström says:

Every new idea must fight for its existence, and find 'space' among the synaptic connections to survive. It is actually the same 'survival-of-the-fittest' conditions as in the physical world that are applied to the world of ideas. I call it 'Neurodarwinism'. The competition in the inner realms of synapses and memory patterns is enormous so that chances of survival are very small. The best way to make it stay is to make the ideas or the words you want to remember unique in some way. That will literally make an impression!

A way of exploring Matti Bergström's results is to use methods where you become aware of the flow of thoughts and ideas in your brain. That is what the rest of this book is about.

brainstorming

Brainstorming is a well-known technique, used to generate new ideas in many situations: product development, marketing, advertising, business development and many more.

We have just learned the results of Matti Bergström's brain research on creativity. The brain seems to work as an idea generator all the time, although we are not aware of it. New forms are created continuously and it is a matter of being in the right state of mind to pick up a few.

In brainstorming it is the flow of random ideas, coming from a group of people, stimulating each other, that is valuable. If you put any restrictions on that flow you risk missing ideas which could have turned out to be the best ones. You never know what you are going to use, that's why you should not make any limitations.

When do you get your best ideas? You get ideas all the time, but some situations are better than others. When asked about it most people say they get their best ideas when they are relaxed – 'just before I fall asleep', 'when I sit in my favourite chair doing nothing', 'when I am in the bath'; if they are doing something where they function automatically – jogging, washing, cooking, doing the dishes, cleaning, knitting, cycling, 'driving my car to work'; or in interaction with other people – coffee/tea-breaks, evening classes, group work.

They very seldom mention situations such as: 'meetings', 'at school' or 'at work'. In those situations they are very much occupied with routine work or, as in the case of meetings, there is a set formula for how things should be handled and you are not expected to put forward any new ideas!

laboratory intelligence and intelligence in the wild

laboratory intelligence

The Swiss researcher Jean Piaget once suggested that we should regard intelligence as something we use when we don't know what to do. For a long time intelligence has been regarded as something we have inherited, a personal skill or ability that is measurable and practically fixed through life – we get what we get and cannot do anything about it. Tests were constructed to measure people's intelligence (IQ, Intelligence Quotient). Any ordinary IQ test mainly contains questions and problems that test a person's ability to solve *mathematical-logical* problems (often series of numbers, omitted figures etc), *spatial* problems (judging similarities of form, position etc) and *linguistic* problems (synonyms, the meaning of words etc).

A logical problem might look like this:

$$\frac{\text{Forest}}{\text{Tree}} = \frac{\text{City}}{?}$$

Which of the following words would you use instead of the question mark above?

a) house
b) bacteria
c) people
d) streets

What would be your answer? Give reasons for your choice.

I choose...

Because:..
....
....

David Perkins, the co-director of Project Zero at Harvard University calls this type of intelligence 'laboratory intelligence'. It is being used for reproduction of facts, to get the 'correct' answer, to show that the person who is being tested has understood the context of the test. In that way it is a rather predictable, not to say programmed type of intelligence that is being tested here. It actually says very little about the person's ability to solve problems in the real world.

'intelligence in the wild'

A type of intelligence that is more practical in everyday life, which consists of a great number of unpredictable situations, could be called 'intelligence in the wild'. When something unforeseen occurs, what do you do?

Let us say you are in a marketplace in a foreign country. Suddenly you become aware of a lot of noise around you, people start screaming, some of them run away and others become very upset and shout in a language you don't understand at all. You become very worried and you don't understand what is going on around you. You don't know how to interpret what is happening. Should you leave? Is something dangerous about to take place? Has anything happened and in that case what? A lot of questions pop up inside you but you have no discernable pattern to help you make sense of the events.

It is in situations like this that you will be able to use your 'intelligence in the wild' but there are certain criteria:

1) It is most important that you become aware of the fact that something is about to happen, that you are *alert to changes*, that you are able to trace events that could lead to danger, etc.

2) You need a certain *attitude to promote this sense of alertness*, so that you notice patterns and events in the surroundings.

3) You also need an *ability to make sense of what you have been observing*, you need knowledge and skills to handle it.

Let's take another example from everyday life. You are supposed to cook a certain dish and you start mixing the ingredients. Suddenly you become aware of the fact that one important ingredient is missing. What do you do then? Are you the type of person who would prefer to follow the recipe strictly? Would you then run off to a grocery store to buy the missing ingredient? Or would you rather start thinking about a possible way to substitute it with something else? Are you a person who normally solves problems 'on the run'? The intelligence in the wild will take over and you will very often find more than one possible solution to the problem.

learning maps

The thinking process is a very chaotic and confusing one. Thoughts don't follow a straight, logical path. They are the result of some million chemical processes among the brain cells each second. Thoughts follow many streams at the same time, making leaps, following a sideline and then returning to the mainstream again.

If you take notes in a traditional, linear way you have to force your thinking into a logical format that is unnatural and will hamper the production of ideas. On the other hand, if you take notes in the form of a learning map you will follow the natural thinking process and make leaps when your thoughts leap. It is also very easy to add new information on lines anywhere in the map.

Here is an example:

Start by defining your subject. Then write the word or draw a symbol for it in the middle of the paper. Let's use the word 'apple' as a starting-point.

Apple

Around this starting-point you then draw lines and write one word on each. Let the information flow for five to six minutes and follow the directions of your thoughts whichever way they take. Write down as many words as possible.

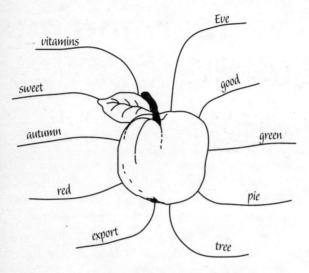

Finally you will end up having a lot of words ranging around your starting-point. By not restricting or structuring the flow of thoughts you have been able to take down a lot of words that would otherwise have been censored before they reached the conscious level in your brain. Once there they can contribute to the process of finding new ideas, new ways of putting the words, combining them with other words in the map to create new images. You have now created a **map of possibilities.**

This is what the map may look like after four or five minutes of free association:

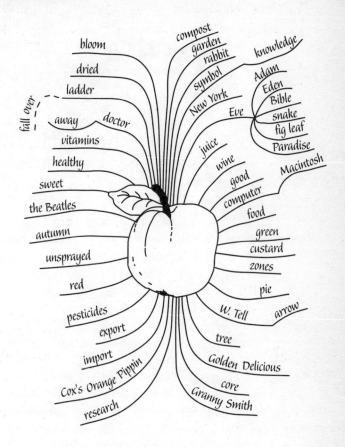

▪ Add new words to the existing branches by drawing out 'twigs' after the subheading. Write down as many words as you think you need to be able to recall the content. The point is, by choosing **the right word** and using a **limited number** of words you will be able to remember more. Each word should contain a lot of the associations and facts you need when you talk about apples. The words will open up like flower buds and give you all the information you need.

Maybe a completed learning map on 'apple' will look like this:

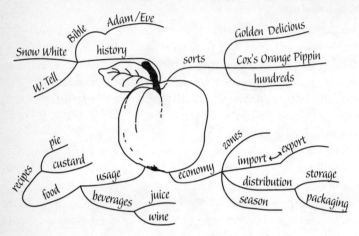

Let's go further and use this map of the word 'apple'. The next phase in the process is to use logical thinking in order to find a structure, to make a choice of words and find suitable connections.

- ■ Pick one word, the word you feel is the most natural to start with, and highlight it.
- ■ Then pick out four, five, six words, you can use as sub-headings in the structure. Those words are often of a general, comprehensive nature. If you cannot find such words in the map, make some new ones up! Write them on the lines as you can see below – one on each line. Try to limit the number of headings. Four to six should be sufficient.

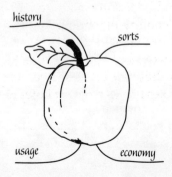

the use of keywords

The funny thing with these maps is that no one will resemble another in spite of the fact that you may all have the same starting-point, the same text, the same lecture, and still the maps will be totally different from one person to another. This is perfectly natural as we all are different, we think differently, have different experiences and knowledge, we have different backgrounds, etc.

As a result of this, when you develop your own personal style you will find you can easily recall the information, the words and the pictures your map contains.

Most people take down too many words in linear, 'normal' notes, which inevitably leads to problems. It takes more time to revise the notes and to find the structure in them. Linear notes are related to time, which means the information is recorded depending on when you read or heard it. There is no easy way of putting information from one part in context with information from other parts.

Using learning maps you will notice you need to remember very few words. Concentrate on **the right words,** those that lead to a better recall. Finding these right words or **keywords** is a skill you develop using learning maps as your note-taking technique.

The ability to pick out the right keywords determines how well you can assimilate the substance of a book, a lecture, a lesson, a magazine article, etc. If you lack this ability you are less able to find the main points; you have to devote more time to revision and to find important facts in your notes. There are many reasons for practising the ability of finding keywords and limiting the number of words you take down.

Let's compare two people's notes originating from a lecture on the brain, which they both listened to. The person who used ordinary, linear notes has 13 pages of notes looking like this:

The person who used a learning map has one page and considerably fewer notes. That person's notes looked like this:

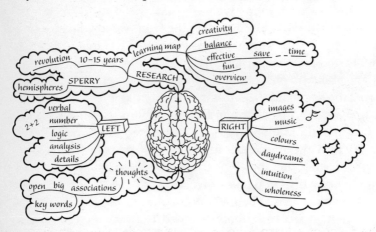

There are more advantages than just the number of words or sheets of paper. I have already mentioned the aspect of time. In linear notes **time** is primary, which also means that I force my brain to use time as a guideline, not the meaning of what I am listening to or reading. If I want to find details in my linear notes I have to think of what I have listened to in a linear or sequential way.

If, on the other hand, I take notes in the form of a learning map, time is irrelevant. In a learning map the content and the meaning are central to the way I take my notes. My notes fork out on lines from an important central point like the branches and twigs of a tree seen from above.

I can add new words anywhere all the time. I can leap from one part to another, make comparisons, follow chronological chains, connect one part with another. As a result there is a well-structured learning map, where lines of association and the meanings of words are clear.

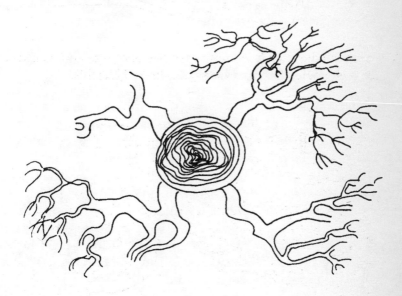

The form of a learning map appeals both to imagination and logical thinking. A learning map is actually a kind of problem-solving and construction work. You start from an idea of what the whole is about and you make a skeleton structure as the main design of the emerging learning map. When you look at it even years later it is this basic design that brings back the meaning.

Using linear notes normally means that you take down the notes in the same order as they appear in the time aspect. However, when using learning maps you sometimes have to wait a while until the speaker or the writer reveals the main ideas, ie the structure you need for your learning map. If you don't have the courage or the nerve to wait until you get that information, start making a draft map, and when you find the real structure you can easily and quickly start on a new learning map, picking out the words you need from the first one.

The alternative is linear notes and the result will be notes as messy as the structure of the speech you are listening to.

Starting with the whole is essential if you want structure and comprehension. Otherwise you get a mixture of important and unimportant facts without a context.

on a memory hunt

A good example of how you can use learning maps is to pull personal memories out of the convolutions of your brain. Begin in the way described above by writing a central word in the middle of a piece of paper and let your thoughts fly away, **but don't forget to write all the time!** With the help of associations you can dig deeper into past events and hidden memories. Even things you have 'forgotten' will find their way up to the surface. It is like pulling in a long line with thousands of hooks, all with fish on them, and taking the fish off the hooks once they come to the surface. But again, it is very important that you write all the time. Otherwise the words will vanish like bubbles in the air.

exercise

Go back in your thoughts to an important event in your life, such as:

■ your childhood
■ your first love
■ your best friend when you were . . . years old
■ an important person in your life
■ the first time you travelled abroad
■ ...

This is how you do it:

■ Write or draw the central word/idea in the middle of a blank piece of paper, for instance, 'My fifth birthday'.
■ Start making free associations to that central point. Let branches and twigs grow out of the centre and write one word on each line. Follow lines of associations as far out as they take you.
■ When you get too many words around the central word, or if your associations suddenly come to an end, just open new 'forks' after one of the existing words.
The important thing is to get as many words as you can, to create an **abundance**.
■ When you have done this for five to ten minutes it is time to stop. Look at all the words and pick out a few that you would like to try on another map. You can either put them in the middle of a new map or just go on writing new associations where the word is in the first map.
Now it is time to go more and more into detail in your associations. It is very important to write down every word that pops into your mind.
■ When you are ready with that stage, let the map rest for a while. The thinking process and the flow of associations will go on in your brain even if you stop writing and when you come back to the map you will have a lot of new words to add. Let the map stay unstructured until you feel it is 'ripe'.

How can you use the map? You can of course let the map stay as it is, but you can also use it for writing down your memories or a story in a linear form.

the natural way

For a long time we have assumed that the brain works in a linear way, which is of course a natural conclusion, judging from the way we speak and write. When we speak the words appear in a correct grammatical order and form most of the time. The same is even more true about our way of writing.

The brain does not normally work in a linear way. For instance, you very seldom remember full sentences from what you read or heard, but rather **single words**.

When you speak, the main part of the energy is used to find the right words, to add a correct grammatical form to the words and to choose from a number of alternatives. It is important not to be misunderstood by using the wrong words or gestures.

At the same time, as you speak and follow a mainstream of thoughts, there is an ongoing process in your brain which not only concerns the mainstream but also several sidetracks, such as: 'Did I turn off the lights before I left?' or 'Those shoes are really ugly!'

You can also easily notice that the listener's brain does not receive your message in a linear way. Often his own associations carry him away to draw conclusions you did not expect. He gets other associations from the same words because he has other experiences connected to them.

As you gradually develop your learning map technique you will notice your **memory and learning skills** develop also. Learning maps and memory techniques are based on the same type of thinking, where you use unique pictures or words to stimulate your **imagination** and **creative thinking**. You **save time** and become more efficient in your listening and reading. You also save time when you revise your notes as they don't consist of a lot of unnecessary words.

If you write the keywords in long rows, as most books on study skills recommend, you miss the opportunity of pointing out connections and getting new ideas.

There is an underlying structure in every text, a skeleton construction. The writer has had a purpose for his text when he wrote it and he has chosen a suitable form for it. Some writers are very clear and help the reader to get the message. Others are vague and difficult to understand. Whatever the writer's style is, learning maps are an excellent note-taking technique to catch the message.

your own writing and speech

When asked about their methods, writers say that the writing process is a matter of at least two separate steps that sometimes conflict with each other: one **productive** and **creative** phase, often **subconscious**, and another **monitoring, editing, censoring** and very **conscious** phase.

Most of us were well trained at school to use the latter phase but not the first. By becoming aware of this dual nature of your way of thinking you can start using the creative side much more. This will increase your ability to write and speak in a more original and personal way.

The language area is located in the left hemisphere, the same hemisphere that is concentrated on structure and details. If we relied only on the language area in the left hemisphere our way of writing would be full of jargon, stereotyped and in a rather bloodless style, far from the potential of the brain.

Learning maps involve imagination as well as structure, pictures as well as logic. In the exercise on page 37 you will practise a method for developing your own writing.

The brain, like many other vital organs in the body, has a vast overcapacity. Everywhere in nature there is abundance. Think of the number of seeds a tree or plant produces and how few of those get an opportunity to develop.

The principle is: **first abundance – then a choice.**

Creativity is really the same thing. By using many possibilities you can later make a choice of the most suitable in order to solve a certain problem or create a new idea.

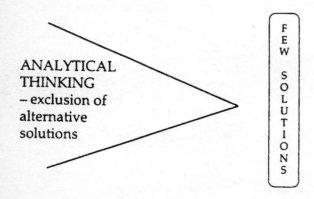

ANALYTICAL
THINKING
– exclusion of
alternative
solutions

FEW SOLUTIONS

By thinking strictly analytically you tend to exclude all suggestions other than those that most obviously solve the problem.

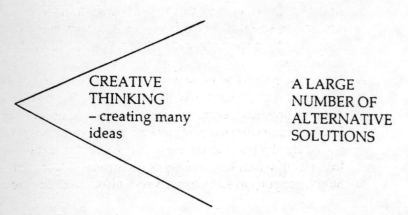

CREATIVE
THINKING
– creating many
ideas

A LARGE
NUMBER OF
ALTERNATIVE
SOLUTIONS

In reality people can't be divided into two groups – those who are analytical and those who are creative. It is rather a question of being both, perhaps with a dominance of one or the other. Most people are trained to be analytical. Creative suggestions are often censored in the process that leads to the final solution.

It is necessary to separate these two ways of thinking. The model we are going to use starts with a creative phase and is followed by an analytical phase:

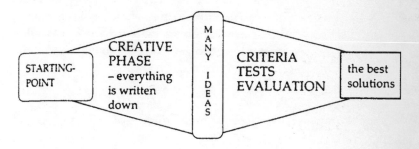

This is how you start:

- ■ Start with the **central word**, a problem, a headline.
- ■ Put the word or a picture **in the middle** of a blank sheet of paper. Use colours to highlight it and make it clear.
- ■ Let your **associations** flow freely for five to ten minutes. Don't try to make a structure at this stage or to censor the words.
- ■ **Write** down every word that comes into your mind.
- ■ If you get stuck, open a new 'fork' anywhere, by drawing out new lines from existing words. It is very important to keep the associations flowing all the time. If you don't, you can easily slip into a structured way of thinking and then lose a lot of words that could give you brilliant ideas later.
- ■ Stop when you have a feeling it is enough or at a fixed time.

Most people don't allow new ideas into the writing process naturally because there is no natural way of including those ideas, especially if the ideas come at the wrong stage. By using a learning map you can add new words all the time. If you make a structure too early you get fewer words and you tend to come up with only 'old' words, ie words that are normally connected to that subject. It is better to start with uncertainty and chaos in your thoughts and let the structure emerge later in the process.

Surprising things happen when you allow your thoughts to drift and it is always interesting to see the result.

Let me show you an example. After having lived in Iceland for some time I was invited to a meeting to give a talk on that country. If I had used the 'normal' way of preparing such a talk it would have taken me a couple of hours to get ready. By using a learning map it took me less than 20 minutes.

This is how I did it:

1. I drew a map of Iceland in the middle of a blank piece of paper.
2. Free associations for five minutes.

This is what the map looked like after those five minutes:

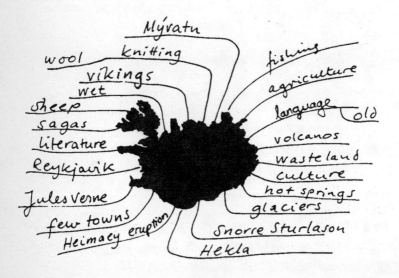

3. I then highlighted a word that was suitable as a starting-point.

4. I took five minutes to talk to someone about the subject. Reason? You think one thing, you write a second and you say a third! The person who was listening added information, asked me questions to open up or explain things that were not clear, etc. In short, it gave me an opportunity to get more ideas about the subject and add those words to my map.

    Another thing that happened during those five minutes of talking was that I got a fairly good idea about a possible structure.

5. I looked at the map more thoroughly and picked out words that could be grouped together and then I tried to find sub-headings for those groups. I 'invented' words that were not in the map. In the process I used my coloured pens to mark the various categories.

This is what the map looked like at that stage:

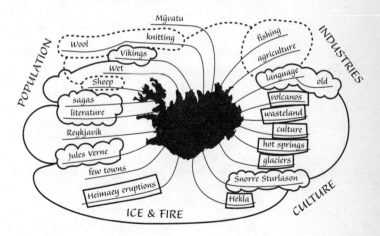

6. I decided which words I should use as sub-headings on the thick branches in my learning map.

7. I took a piece of blank paper and drew a new map of Iceland in the middle. Around the centre I drew six lines which are the thick branches and I added all the other words – **no more no less** – I thought I might need during the speech. I added pictures where pictures could replace words.
8. I used my coloured pens to highlight, decorate or define the groups of words.

This is the final learning map *and* the manuscript of my speech. This took less than 20 minutes. When you go through the same process from idea to a manuscript the first time it might take a lot longer but each time you do it you get better and better.

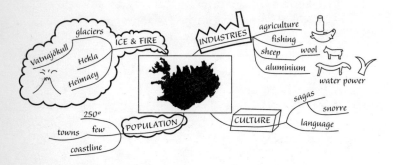

I can still add or change anything in the learning map, even make another structure very quickly by rewriting it. When I finally give my speech I can add or delete words, change the order of the 'chapters' or make any changes I like even in the last minute before I start talking.

exercise

Imagine you are going to give a speech to a group of people and you are allowed to choose a subject of your own. It could be anything from 'Economic planning in Indonesia' to 'My summer holidays in 1997'.

Go through the same steps as described above and in the learning map on page 41.

Learning map for exercise on page 40

You go through the same steps for anything that comes out of your head to be used for speeches, writing, personal planning, projects, problem solving – anything that involves your own knowledge or feelings.

This model is also excellent for use in groups. It works the same way but takes longer, especially the brainstorming session.

style

When you learn a new way of doing things it is common for old habits to be retained and interfere with the new. With learning maps it will show in the number of words you take down and in the way you write the words or draw your mind maps.

With practice you will discover the ways that suit your thinking and how your memory works. Develop your own personal style. If you like to draw pictures and use colour pens a lot, do so! If you remember better with words and with only a few colours added, do so! **It is the result that counts**!

In this chapter I give you some advice, practical hints and a summary of rules. In the learning map on pages 100–101 you get a summary of the whole book including the rules.

The style I use personally, which is the way the learning maps have been drawn in this book, is the **hayfork model**. I draw lines from the central point and when I want to add more words I draw new lines and write the words on them.

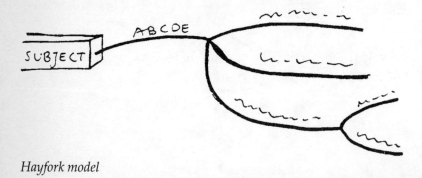

Hayfork model

Of course there are other ways of doing it! I will show you some variations here. Try them and find out which one you like most.

The first looks like this. It is called the **fishbone model.**

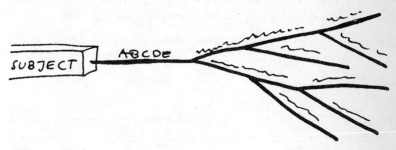

Fishbone model

The second looks like molecules or bubbles, so let's call it **mubbles** (molecular bubbles). It is also called **clustering**.

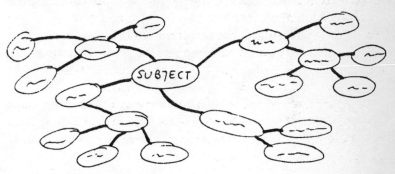

Mubble or clustering

(Warning! Don't write a lot of words in the mubble, not more than one word in each.)

The third variety is not one I can recommend but I see it very often in beginners' maps. It has no name but looks like this:

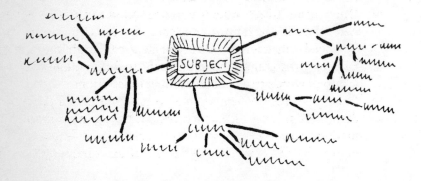

There is a risk of confusion if you put too many words in your learning map. If you write the words close to each other it is sometimes difficult to perceive where they come from. Especially if you use your learning maps for giving speeches or if you assemble a lot of information into one learning map, I advise you to avoid this form. It is just as easy to use the hayfork model where you draw lines and **write on the lines.**

rules

Here are some important rules in learning maps:

- ■ **Start in the middle of the paper**. If you use A4 sheets turn them sideways. It is easier to spread out the lines that way and to read what you have written. It is a frequent beginner's fault to turn the paper round as you write. Don't do that! It takes a lot of time to read the words when you use the learning map later on.
- ■ **Print the words** – it makes it easier to read!
  Use mainly lower case but if you like you can use CAPITALS now and then, for instance to show the

important words or the keywords in your map. It is easier to read lower case as the words differ more from one another than capital letters.

■ **One word on each line**. If you need more words, draw new lines. Try to limit the number of words you write. You need only a few words if you choose the right ones.

■ **Use colours** to highlight, to decorate, to differentiate one group of words from another and in illustrations.

■ **Draw pictures**. Pictures contain a lot more information than words. Try to find pictures that can gather information from a whole group of words. In the learning map at the end of this book you will see examples of this.

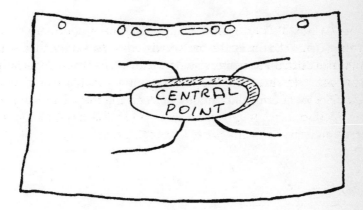

■ Use **symbols, signs** and **arrows** to show connections in your learning map or if you want to refer to other material such as quotations, graphs, charts and other reference material you don't want to have in the learning map.

■ **Make details in your learning map unique**. Every learning map is in itself unique, but you can, for instance, make some of the words, pictures and symbols stand out in some respect by drawing them three-dimensional.

The reason for this is of course that uniqueness is a way of increasing your memory power.

■ **Use your imagination!** Nothing is really forbidden in your own learning map. A learning map is a personal note-taking technique and whatever increases your use of it is permitted. As simple as that!

other people's texts

When you make a learning map from other people's texts the perspective is different. Now you cannot walk through the same phases as when you write your own texts. When you work with other people's texts you have to uncover someone else's thoughts and analyse how he has put the structure together. This way of looking at a text needs a completely different strategy.

The writer has created an order of her own out of a chaotic non-structure, but you have to start with the result in its more or less well-structured appearance. Using traditional note taking with keywords, underlining or highlighting words, etc will only let you stay on the surface. To achieve a full understanding of the text you have to get below the surface.

The learning map technique will allow you to get in very close contact with the depth structure of the text, as it is implied in that technique that you start with the underlying structure and add the details. This closeness to the writer will be very revealing – a bad writer just as well as a good writer will be revealed in a merciless way when you get so close to their way of thinking.

The reader, using learning maps, will very quickly learn to appreciate this new way of approaching a text.

The first step is to get an overview, ie to get an idea of the wholeness of the text and not primarily the details. We will now use the following method.

Follow these steps:

1. Why do I read this text?
2. 'Read' to get an overview
3. Type of text
4. Prepare a learning map
5. Read again
6. Rewrite your learning map

making an overview

why do I read this text?

The answer to that question determines how much time you should devote to the text. It also determines **how many** words you pick out from the text and **what** those words are.

'read' to get an overview

short articles, magazines, etc
If you have a short article of just a few pages, read the whole article from the beginning to the end. To 'read' means that you read through the text very quickly without stopping at details. Your aim is to grasp the general idea. It is an advantage if you read with a highlighter in your hand, marking the words that seem to be important. This is only to prepare your mind so the next time you read the text these words are already familiar to you and they help you to grasp the wholeness of the text quicker.

longer texts, books, etc
A longer text must be treated differently. If you want to summarize a whole book do this:

■ Look at the table of contents
■ Read the text on the jacket

▦ Read preface and summaries
▦ Flick through the whole book. Look at every page, especially: words in **bold**, *italics*, words that are <u>underlined</u> and other typographical ways of telling the reader what is important in a text.

Information like that is often very valuable. Someone has prepared the text for the reader to help him understand it better.

▦ Use a highlighter while reading as described above in order to catch important keywords.
▦ Let this part of the process take up to one third of the actual reading time.

Why read the text this way first? It is very important you reach a level of understanding the text as a whole, its purpose and contents, what is new and what you know already. If you know what the wholeness is about it is much easier to get hold of the important details later.

type of text

Before making a learning map you have to find a suitable design for each specific text. All texts are different and thus all designs are different. Making a learning map is in many ways the same thing as problem solving. You get to know the structure of a text when reading it through but most people do not know what to look for. Getting information out of a text of any length is to most people a random process. The way we have been taught study skills traditionally does not help enough if you really want to understand and remember the contents of a text.

However, when you start using learning maps it is natural for you to look for the type and design of a text in order to find a suitable first design for your learning map. You can easily understand why you have to start with a conception of the wholeness. If the type of text is not evident you must still choose a design to start with. It is easy to redraw once you find a more suitable design.

To make it simple can most texts could be categorized into three groups:

1. Comparisons
2. Chronologies or chains of events
3. Presentations

comparisons
This is when the text is divided into **either ... or**, when **a** is compared to **b** and maybe **c**, when one is good and the other bad ... and so forth.

The design of the learning map could for instance look like this:

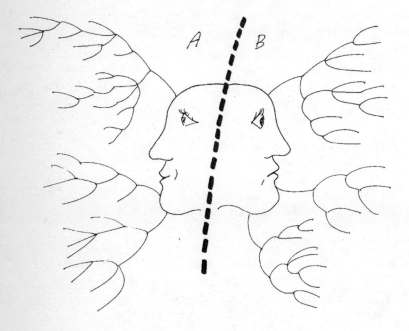

chronologies or chains of events
Something has a clear beginning and an end, eg biographies, history, processes, manuals ...

The easiest way to make a learning map with this design is to follow the clock.

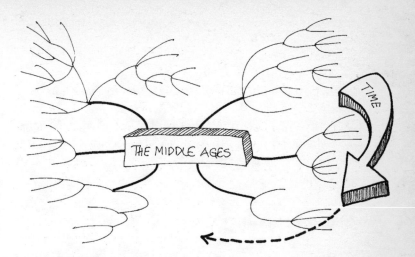

presentations

... which will be the rest! When a story is told without a clear beginning or end, when facts are being presented without specific or necessary order, you may start wherever you like. Details must be reorganized from the text into your own order as you have chosen in your design.

Of course you will find mixed texts – there will be comparisons and chronologies mixed with presentations but you must still choose a main feature as your design, depending on your own understanding of the text. In that case let comparisons and chronologies be a natural part of the branches and twigs in your learning map.

No two people will ever make identical learning maps! That is important to bear in mind as there is no 'correct' way of doing it but there are more or less suitable ways. A learning map that works is one that works **for you!**

prepare a learning map

read again

These two last steps will be presented together as they are inter-woven in your work with the text.

When you have read or flicked through a text or a book you will have a rough understanding of the wholeness. You will also have found out what type of text you are reading. Now it is time to prepare a learning map.

You write down the first design, starting in the middle and branching a few main keywords. These are the 'hooks' and while reading the text more carefully this second time you make new branches and twigs and pine needles, adding details into your learning map, just as described earlier in this book.

This process of reading and taking down important keywords is interwoven. You read a passage – add new words into your learning map – read a passage – add words … until you have dealt with the whole text.

rewrite your learning map

Always rewrite your learning map even if you are happy with it. Every time you rewrite it you revise the material and you get rid of words you already know, words that are superfluous in one way or another.

Rewriting, redesigning, mean revision and learning.

using learning maps

One aspect of using learning maps is when you start with your own ideas and knowledge. Let's call it 'note making'. The other aspect is 'note taking', ie when you are trying to organize your notes from texts, speeches, etc that someone else has prepared. When you use learning maps in connection with learning, making summaries, analyses or any other type of note-taking function, you will use skills you have learned already in this book although some parts of the method may be different.

Finding keywords, getting overview and wholeness, the way you make the learning map graphically, using both imagination and logic, are just as important when we turn to the note-taking aspect of learning maps.

When you read a text, whether it is a book or a short magazine article, this is a method you can use:

- First, **flick through** the whole text very **quickly** to get a idea of the contents. Use a highlighter while you are skimming through the text and **mark** words you think are important. It does not really matter if you are going to use them later or not.
- **Prepare a learning map** by drawing/writing the central point and a couple of the main branches. Write a few words/subheadings, one on each line.

■ **Decide why you are reading that text.** The purpose is important because it determines the number of words and which individual words you pick out of the text as keywords. Do you read it for pleasure, to learn to make a summary or a report for someone else, or what is the purpose?

■ **Read** through the whole text and **add keywords** to your learning map. You will find the quick first glance has been quite significant. It is amazing how much you pick up and how quickly you can note it.

■ **Rewrite your learning map** and decide what to keep and what to get rid of. Only use the words you need to remember the contents!
Very often the structure of the text is not clear before you have made your first learning map. That is one of the reasons why I recommend you rewrite it. The other important reason is that every time you rewrite it you learn by repetition and you are able to exclude more and more words because you have learned what the text is about. The goal in any learning process is to get the information into your head and make it stay there!

On the following pages you will find two exercises where you can apply the method just described. The first text is about fasting and the second is about McDonald's.

Here is first a learning map to summarize what has just been said about using learning maps:

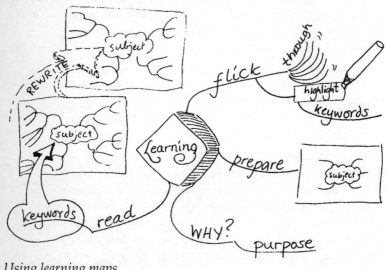

Using learning maps

text 1: fasting

'Why are you fasting if you don't have to lose weight?', people ask me when I have been fasting. To most people the only reason for fasting is to lose weight. Fasting is of course an excellent way of losing weight too, but it is not the main reason for doing it.

When you are fasting the metabolism in your body is changed. Your body gets rid of dross products that have gathered during the years. You re-establish a natural balance. Normally you lose weight too, but most of it is a loss of water which you will regain when you start eating again as usual.

When you don't feel well or are feverish you fast sponta-neously. Most animals fast at times and so do human beings in most cultures.

The safest way to fast is to use herbal teas and juice from raw fruits or vegetables. It is easy to produce these raw juices in your own home. Many people prefer fasting in a group, where they can support each other. If you suffer from any illnesses you should only fast according to your doctor's recommendation.

Most juices and herbal teas taste good, but if you dislike any of them, try others.

It is very important that you are mentally prepared for your fasting period and that you have decided to do it of your own free will. You can also prepare yourself by eating less 'heavy' food the week before you start. The day before you start you should eat only raw fruit and vegetables.

During the fasting period you only drink juices made from fresh fruit, berries or vegetables, and herbal teas. If you can, get clean mineral water (not carbonated). You should drink between two and three litres of lukewarm water, juice or tea every day. It is quite a lot of liquid to drink every day and you feel you are drinking something all the time. But on the other hand, you don't feel hungry. It's the habit and social side of eating you will miss most.

You should of course avoid 'poisons' such as coffee, ordinary tea, tobacco and alcohol. The cleaner your body gets, the more sensitive it becomes. Besides, it is rather pointless to ruin the good effects of the fasting process by bringing new poisons into the body to replace those you got rid of!

It's very important to keep your stomach going. You must get rid of all the dross. It if stays in your intestines or in your stomach, you may start feeling bad. You can use various sorts of herbs that will keep your stomach working.

When I fast I keep on working as usual, but I normally start during a weekend. I feel well all the time. A reason for not being among people too much is that your body doesn't smell so good from the dross products! You should always do some exercise during the fasting period. Especially if you don't feel well it's important that you keep moving instead of going to bed.

When you end the fasting period, you must be very careful about what you eat. For the first breakfast you can eat half an apple. You will be amazed how little you will need to feel satisfied! For lunch you can have some vegetable soup and for dinner some raw vegetables. And you keep on drinking the same sorts of juice as before. The next day you add some cottage cheese and yoghurt, and you keep on adding a little extra every day. If you eat too much you can end up having terrible pains in your stomach.

During this period you have a very good opportunity of changing your eating habits. Your body is as clean as ever. It's a radical experience and you can feel how important it is that you eat the right things.

After the fasting period you feel strong and happy that you did it.

comments on text 1

Now that you have read the text and marked a few keywords it is time to decide what the learning map is going to look like. Begin by drawing a picture in the middle of a sheet of paper, symbolizing 'fasting'. Make a circle or a box around it.

If you want to make the learning map entirely without help, don't read further until you have finished your own learning map.

At the beginning of the text you are given two **motives** for fasting: **losing weight** and **getting rid of dross products** in your body. Put 'motives' on a thick branch and the other two on twigs drawn out from the branch. Add other words after these two on new lines.

Other branch words you can use are, for instance: **preparations, method, how to end**.

Draw pictures wherever it is appropriate, use colours, arrows and other signs, highlight important words.

comments on text 2

Text 2 is very different in its construction from text 1. The story of the McDonald's chain of restaurants is a chronological account of how it all started and later developed. There are also remarks on the business idea, which you have to take into the learning map somehow. Look for the main keywords the first time you read it and build the learning map clockwise, using events and years as your structure.

text 2: McDonald's

The practices pioneered and perfected by McDonald's have revolutionized the food service industry and changed eating habits throughout the world. Some 96 per cent of American consumers have eaten at one of McDonald's restaurants during the past year. More than half the American population live within a three-minute drive of a McDonald's restaurant. There are more than 9300 McDonald's restaurants and they handle 17 per cent of all restaurant visits in the United States. McDonald's sells 32 per cent of all hamburgers sold by commercial restaurants and 26 per cent of all french fries in the US.

McDonald's is said to be America's largest job-training organization and one out of every 15 American workers got his or her first job there. Moreover, there are McDonald's in many other countries. Today it is one of the best known – perhaps *the* best known – exponent of American culture.

Yet the story of McDonald's is not very old. It all started in 1954 when Ray Kroc, a 51-year-old entrepreneur, met Maurice (Mac) and Richard (Dick) McDonald in San Bernadino, some 60 miles east of Los Angeles on the edge of the desert. Ray Kroc, who dropped out of school from boredom in the 10th grade, was very enterprising, outgoing and open. During World War I, when he was 15 years old, he lied about his age and volunteered to become a Red Cross ambulance driver in the same company as another under-aged driver by the name of Walt Disney.

Kroc, who had his home in Chicago, was a food service equipment salesman. For many years he sold paper cups, and later acquired the national marketing rights to Multimixers, which were used to make milk shakes. Many hotel bars and lounges, which had lost business through Prohibition, were serving various ice cream and dairy drinks.

The McDonald brothers left New England and moved to California at the time of the Depression. By the mid-1930s cars were becoming a vital part of the new lifestyle. As California weather was warm, drive-ins were introduced and in 1937 the McDonald brothers opened their first tiny drive-in eating place. Three years later they opened a much grander drive-in in San Bernadino, which was becoming a working-class boomtown.

By the mid-1940s the McDonald's drive-in had become the town's most popular teenage hang-out. Although their business was lucrative, the McDonald brothers saw the changes that were taking place. The trend was to reduce staff and to limit the choice of products. They closed their drive-in for three months in the autumn of 1948 and adapted it to the fast-food market. They cut the menu from 25 items to nine, and their kitchen crew became specialized; two people were assigned to make milk shakes all day.

The McDonald brothers' drive-in got a lot of attention from people in the business. In fact, before the historical meeting with Ray Kroc, they had 15 franchises. The brothers had a thriving business but they wanted to take life somewhat more leisurely. A week after their first meeting, Kroc called from Chicago to say that he wanted to negotiate a contract that would give him exclusive rights to franchise the McDonald system nationally.

In 1955 Kroc planned his own McDonald's on the outskirts of Chicago, not far from his home. He soon discovered, however, that there were numerous problems in transferring a McDonald's from southern California to the Midwest. The structure was designed without a basement, but Kroc needed space for a furnace to heat the restaurant during Chicago winters. He also needed somewhere to put the potatoes as he could not leave them outdoors the way the McDonald's in California did. Ventilation was also a problem.

In 1961, Ray Kroc asked to buy out the McDonald brothers. They replied that their price was $2.7 million – in cash in one lump sum. That would give each of the brothers $1 million and leave $700,000 to cover the taxes. It was a very high price, but Kroc was getting more and more desperate. He wanted to get rid of the brothers.

Shortly after Ray Kroc accepted the price he learned from the brothers that their San Bernardino store was not included in the deal. Kroc was furious. As a result, when the agreement was finalized, Kroc flew to Los Angeles and bought a piece of property only one block from the McDonald brothers' store with the intention of running them out of business.

When Kroc's new McDonald's opened, Kroc forced the brothers to take down their McDonald's sign and many old customers started going to Kroc's new McDonald's in the belief that it was replacing the old restaurant.

Kroc wanted to establish a fast-food business that was characterized by uniformity and quality service and products. His genius was building a system that required all its members to maintain the same standards. A McDonald's was always a McDonald's no matter where it was located.

(Extract from *Americans and the US* by Frederic Fleisher, Seminarium 1987)

what is the memory?

'What help is a memory to me when I don't know my own name, when I wouldn't recognise my own signature, even if you put it right under my nose. I have forgotten it all!

'That's the whole point! In order to give you a new fantastic future we first had to wipe away your past. We must release your cortex from all memories if you are to acquire new skills.'

This quotation is taken from the book *A Living Soul*, by the Swedish writer P C Jersild, and we shall use it as a starting-point to a short discussion on the nature of memory.

The main character in Jersild's book is a brain, which has been put in an aquarium, left with its ears to paddle with and its eyes. Scientists are using it for experiments. Now and then it is given electric shocks in order to extinguish all traces of past memories. However much they try, there are still bits and pieces left.

Then where is the memory located and how does it function? Answer: No one knows! The memory seems to be everywhere and nowhere.

the brain as a hologram

A theory put forward by the American Karl Pribram (and others) is the so-called 'Hologram Theory'. A hologram is a kind of three-dimensional picture. An ordinary photo depicts an object in a way that a brain can interpret. If there is a horse on it, that is what we see. It is not possible to interpret a holographic plate from what we actually see. All we can see is a mass of patterns. However, if we let laser light hit it, we can see a three-dimensional object protrude on the other side of the plate.

The interesting thing about a hologram is that every little piece of the plate could recreate the whole. If we tear an ordinary photo of a horse to pieces, we will get as many pieces of the horse as we tear apart. If we break a holographic plate into pieces, every piece will still recreate the whole horse – but the smaller the piece we have, the weaker the picture will be.

Is it the same way with the brain, that the memory is distributed all over the brain and all of it in every single cell?

memory patterns

There have been many theories through the ages about the nature of the memory and where it is located. Aristotle was of the opinion that the memory was placed in a person's heart, while his thinking process was going on in his head.

Plato's theory that the memory was like a *tabula rasa* (a clean slate) has lasted throughout the course of history. He said that impressions were carved on to a wax tablet, just as an artist engraves his motifs with a sharp instrument.

This theory resembles what we know about 'engrams' or 'memory patterns'. Impressions create lasting patterns in the nerve system of the brain, which is the reason why we can remember.

Most memory researchers agree that memories are stored in the cortex of the brain.

Interesting experiments have been carried out to transfer memory chemically. RNA (Ribonucleic acid) was transferred from one animal to another and it turned out that one animal actually 'inherited' memories from the other.

If memory could be transferred chemically, could it also be inherited genetically, from one generation to another?

in the beginning there was an image

A lot of people compare the human memory with that of a computer, but there are considerable differences. The computer memory is built up in a hierarchical model – there is primary and secondary information on different levels – as in computer software, where you go from one module to another, from one menu to another, finding your way to more specific details. The human memory is not a flowchart as in the computer. The way a computer works implies that it has to search through its whole memory in order to find what has been asked for, while the brain works in a completely different manner. Substantial parts of the brain's information handling instead imply images, feelings, smells, colours and associations of various kinds. Parts can make up wholes and the other way round. We normally don't remember in words, but in images, inner pictures which become words at later stages in the process. Memories could perhaps be split up and stored as parts of a complex situation, but when they are retrieved they form a whole again.

does memory degenerate with increasing age?

When we get older our mental agility is decreased. This means that our ability to react in various situations is changed with increasing age, not dramatically, but there is a change. We get slower, up to 20 to 30 per cent slower between the ages of 20 and 80 years. This is probably due to chemical changes in the nerve cells of the brain and in the transmission of the nerve impulses.

Considerable interest has been shown in the memory abilities of elderly people. Tests generally indicate that elderly people have worse results than younger ones, but these tests have mostly been constructed **by** young people, **for** young people with perfect hearing and eyesight. Elderly people are therefore often misjudged in those tests. Given other tests where the same group of people is followed over a period of time, only small or no differences appear between the mental abilities of younger and elderly people. And if there are differences, they often don't appear until advanced age.

We generally think that our mental ability is at a peak at about the age of 20, but our logical ability, for instance, is best at around the age of 30, while our verbal ability is best around 50! Perhaps more people should join adult education?

Disease and mental inactivity have a strong negative influence on intellectual capacity. Those who are active and sharpen their intellect through the years will also keep those functions a lot longer: 'Use it or you lose it!'

If we speak about memory more specifically we ought to divide it into four separate layers: sensory register, short-term memory, long-term memory and permanent long-term memory.

The **sensory register** is the first memory layer and here we register the information that is taken in through the senses. The time span for this layer is very short. The information is either 'accepted' and channelled further into the system or rejected. The sensory register seems to be unchanged throughout our lives and does not deteriorate with increasing age.

In the **short-term memory** we store what we need temporarily, for instance a phone number. We keep it in our short-term memory as long as we need it, which could be some 10 to 20 seconds or up to a couple of minutes and then it disappears or is transferred to the long-term memory for storage. Between five and seven digits seem to be what we can normally handle without having to write them down. Short-term memory does not appear to be affected by increasing age either.

Long-term memory is, as the term suggests, a layer for long-term storage. It is very important how we code the information when we let it in to this layer. If we give it the wrong code the information will be difficult to retrieve. The capacity of this layer does change with age, but it could also be influenced by training. Later we shall see the wonders memorizing techniques can do to improve long-term memory.

Elderly people seem to have more problems than younger ones in retrieving information from this layer. The causes are probably to be found in the chemical change processes in the nerve system. It normally takes a little longer for an older person to remember than for a younger person.

Elderly people have as good a memory as younger people when it comes to recognizing things, particularly if they make use of cues. Younger people could more easily repeat in detail what they have learned, while elderly people more easily remember principles, overview and wholeness and often forget about details. Details could always be found if you need them!

Many elderly people say that they can more easily remember things that happened long ago while recent events are more

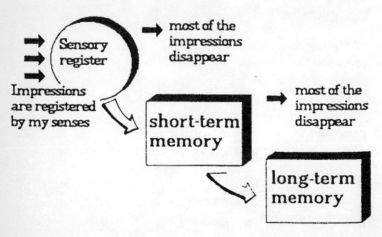

difficult to remember. There is, however, no proof whatsoever that the **permanent long-term memory** should improve with increasing age. Most elderly people don't experience much change in their everyday routines so there are very few new things to remember.

Ageing seems to have very little effect on the ability to remember. Illness, however, has an influence, but the normal healthy ageing process does not stop anyone from learning new things all their lives!

exercise

Before continuing, you could test your own memory with this list of words. Read carefully and slowly through the list once and try to remember as many words as possible. Then answer the questions on the next page – without looking back at this page, of course!

sun	sweat
pen	see
four	two
and	advantage
see	lawn
machine	shoe
two	blanket
ship	guitar
tomato	fish
see	entry
perfume	several
Queen Elizabeth	label
for	ink
sausage	street
automatically	liver

Write down all the words that you remember from the list above. It does not matter if it is in the same order.

_____

_____

_____

_____

Compare your list with the original one.
How many of the first few words did you remember?
And how many of the last five words?

_____

_____

Which words appeared more than once?

_____

_____

Did any words stand out as being totally different from the rest?

_____

_____

the 'von Restorff effect'

Usually one remembers better from the **beginning** of the list and from the **end** of the list, also words that are **repeated** and words that **differ** in one way or another from the rest. This effect is called the 'von Restorff effect'.

These conclusions are worth noticing, especially if you are a person who writes articles, gives speeches or leads meetings. The consequences of this little memory test are many. We could, for instance, use coloured markers (highlighters) to indicate important passages or words in a text. We could put most of the important information at the beginning and at the end, and we could use jokes, imagery and other effects to facilitate learning and remembering.

People who differ from others in the way they dress, behave or look, or if they have an unusual name, are easier to remember than others.

one day is like the pearl ...

'One day is like the pearl, the others are like the oyster,' said Captain Onedin in one of his rare soft moments in the TV series, standing on the deck at dawn with his wife. There is much truth in this sentence!

Daily routines are much the same to most people. Routines and habits, at work as well as at home, make most days 'oysters'. If everything is the same way today as it was yesterday, there is nothing special to remember.

As you might have noticed in the memory test on page 67 it is easier to remember words that differ in some way (*Queen Elizabeth*, for instance) or if they are repeated.

The others tend to become blurred. That is also why many people can't remember what they had for lunch last week – unless something unusual was attached to it.

If we don't spice our lives with 'pearls', life will be a series of blurred events with a few clear highlights long ago and you end up wondering what happened in **your** life. A lot of people today don't live a life of their own. They let others live it in the maga- zines they read and in the TV programmes they watch. It is not much use going out, because they can't see such beautiful things as they show on telly anyway!

If that is the way you live, more or less, you need strong sensations to make an impact on you. Perhaps that is an explanation of why violence and realism have become more naked on news programmes and in newspapers today. Often the effect will be the opposite: we get used to stronger and stronger sensations and we need more and more to make us react. Too much information will also lead to a deteriorating memory. There is a threshold for under-stimulation as well as over-stimulation.

learning with motivation

Have you thought that it seems easier to learn new things when you are enjoying yourself? If you are bored it takes longer, you will forget more quickly and you must revise more often.

These are well-known facts, as most people have experienced both. With modern scanning techniques it is possible to get pictures of the brain showing the consumption of blood sugar in colours – the higher the consumption, the higher the temperature. From the pictures you could easily confirm your own experiences. The brains that are 'having fun' are mainly coloured yellow, orange, red and green, ie warm colours indicating a high consumption of energy. In a brain that is 'bored' there are a few warm spots, but the dominating colours are green and blue.

This is worth noticing when we talk about learning, memory and forgetting. My mind-set determines what I will do, what I will learn and what I will remember. It is my attitude which most determines my success. A positive attitude gives me a much better chance of achieving success than if I am negative and see everything as boring.

Motivation is the keyword in this context.

different types of memory

There are many kinds of memory. Those which engage our senses are called **sensory**. Here are some examples:

visual	– you remember things you *see*
auditory	– you remember things you *hear*

kinaesthetic	– you remember *movements and feelings*
tactile	– you remember *what you touch with your hands*
taste	– you remember *flavours*
smell	– you remember *scents and smells*

Test yourself with the words below. What memories are evoked?
Try to apply the list above for each word one by one in order to
evoke memories of various kinds. What senses give you the best
result? Write down beside the words the memories you evoke.

raw onion _____

walking on beach _____

whipped cream _____

ice _____

mould _____

a hug _____

a rose _____

playing children _____

(Use more spaces to write elsewhere if you like.)

the threads of memory

The Swedish psychologist Timo Mäntylä has carried out some
interesting experiments on the importance of **cues**. In his thesis
How Do You Cue? he describes how the 'guinea-pigs' created their
own cues to certain words, which they were given to remember in
the test. The result was amazing.

In order to activate the memory we need some sort of trigger
word or cue. You will get these cues talking to someone, in
pictures, notes, free associations, events, places, etc. When you

start creating such cues deliberately you are on your way to using memorizing techniques. It is your ability to create such cues that will determine how well you will be able to recall the words you have learned. If the cue is to be really effective it has to be present at the 'coding' of the new words **and** when you are going to retrieve the information from the long-term memory.

There are certain criteria that a cue should meet: it should be **unique** and you must be able to retrieve it. The cue is connected to the characteristics of the initial word and the associations you get from it.

Timo Mäntylä's experiment showed amazingly good results, even several weeks after the actual test.

In the first the research groups were asked to add three cue words of their own to each word in the test list. They got 20 seconds for each word. If they got the word 'zebra' one person might have written the following words on his list: 'savannah', 'stripes' and 'Africa'. Another person might have written: 'black/white', 'pedestrian crossing' and 'traffic'.

Later, when they were asked to remember the words on the memory list, they were only allowed to look at their own cues. It appeared that the result was as high as 95 per cent and at another control several weeks later the result was just as high again!

When compared with other groups where the participants did not have access to cues, the difference was enormous.

Now let's try the same type of test. On page 105 you will find 30 words. Use about 20 seconds on each word to write down three cues on a piece of paper. When you have done all 30, put the book aside and do something else for a while not thinking about the list of words. After some time take out the cues again – don't look at the words in this book! – and write down as many of the initial 30 words as possible.

Do the same thing once more two or three weeks later and see how many words you remember.

in a nutshell

We can always increase our capacity through **training**.

■ It is **never too late** in life to start training.
■ The potential of the brain is practically **unlimited**.
■ The **von Restorff effect** means we can help our memory by:
  - *exaggerating* what we wish to remember;
  - using *coloured pens* for highlighting when we are reading or making notes of our own;
  - making *associations* to the words we are learning;
  - using *jokes, imagery, striking examples,* etc which will create **unique** pictures in the brain.
■ We learn more easily if we are having **fun** and **appreciate** what we are doing.
■ **Motivation** and a **positive attitude** are factors that strongly influence our ability.
■ If we make more days into **pearls** we will have more things to remember and will live a more fulfilling life.
■ New ideas are created in the clash between **chaos and order** in the brain. We need both these states in our lives in order to develop.
■ **Effective cues** will increase our memory capacity considerably.

mnemonics

Memorizing techniques are not new; they were created thousands of years ago by the Greeks. In Greek mythology there is a goddess called **Mnemosyne.** She is the goddess of memory and is known mainly from the following story:

Mnemosyne had a love affair with Zeus, the highest god in Greek mythology, that lasted for nine days and nine nights. As a result of this love affair Mnemosyne gave birth to nine children – the nine Muses.

The nine Muses are the patron goddesses of the noble arts. Their names are: **Clio, Euterpe, Thalia, Melpomene, Terpischore, Erato, Polyhymnia, Calliope, Urania.** Not all of them are well-known in our day, but you may recognize **Thalia**, the Muse of Comedy, as the patron goddess of the theatre.

A myth is very often knowledge in disguise, because a story is more easily remembered than raw facts. In this case we might interpret the myth as a formula for memorizing techniques. The goddess of memory is united with the highest god Zeus, ie order and energy. As a result they get the nine Muses, who represent creativity and imagination.

So if you want to achieve a better memory you should combine structure with imagination:

order/structure + imagination/creativity = memory

This is the formula for most memorizing techniques, including those that have been constructed in modern times.

the story of Simonides

The Greek poet Simonides had been invited to a party to read his poetry. During the meal Simonides was called to the door, as there was someone to see him outside. When he went outside, the house suddenly fell apart. As it was a stone house, the people inside were instantly killed. Simonides was the only survivor from the party. The relatives of those killed all wanted to know which body was which, so that they could bury the right person and the only one who could help them was Simonides. To everyone's surprise he was able to give them many details of the people who had been inside. He had used a very effective memory technique, putting everything he wanted to remember in a familiar place. This method then made it easy for him to recall everything he had put in each place.

The story of Simonides was told by the Roman statesman and writer Cicero in *De Oratore,* his book on rhetoric. Cicero deals with memorizing techniques as part of rhetoric. To the perfect speaker it was necessary to keep every word of a long speech in his memory, as he was not allowed to use a manuscript. Having a good memory was a sign of being loved by the gods.

In another Roman book, *Ad Herennium,* by an unknown author, we find notes on those factors which strengthen the memory and weaken the memory. We tend to forget things that belong to everyday life more easily than those which are odd and new. By noticing this fact we can add an important element to the art of mnemonics: if we deliberately create mental pictures that are unique and different in some respects, eg ugly, absurd, rude, humorous, sensual, adding colour and life to them, we achieve a near-perfect memory.

Time to practise some memory techniques!

exercise

Read the following numbers and words and try to remember each number and word together. You have one minute.

5	bike	10	frog
9	pistol	7	bottle
3	cucumber	4	cake
6	shoe	2	bird
1	floor	8	truck

Cover the words above and write down as many as you can remember:

1 _____	6 _____
2 _____	7 _____
3 _____	8 _____
4 _____	9 _____
5 _____	10 _____

Well, how did you manage? Normally, it does not work so well the first time, unless you have a functioning memory technique. Would you believe it if you were told you could easily score all ten with one or two more tries? First you will get to know the principles (pages 77–82) and then another exercise, and I can guarantee that most of you who read this book will score all ten next time!

logic and imagination

Most memorizing techniques are based on the same elements, logic and imagination.

Let me use an image to explain what this is all about. You have two piles of paper which you would like to join up to make a book. On one pile you have a logically built up system of rules, often based on figures. On the other pile you find the words you are supposed to remember.

1 2 3 4 Structure 5 6 7 8 9 10	1 2 3 4 Words to 5 remember 6 7 8 9 10

You always learn the rule system by heart, in order to use it for recall of the words you want to remember.

In order to join the two piles you need imagination. With the help of associations you create images that join number one on the pile to the left with number one on the pile to the right. In that way you make a connection that will help you to remember better. You will soon know exactly how this is done.

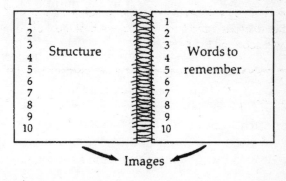

associations

The word association is often mentioned in connection with memory. It is the central element in all memorizing techniques. The word is formed by the Latin word *ad* which means 'to' and *socius* which means 'ally'. So the word 'association' means: 'things that are connected to each other'.

In this instance it means we are trying to find words that are related to our original word. Our associations can be of many kinds. they can be **synonyms**, words that have the same meaning. They can be words that explain or define the original word. But they can also be of another kind altogether, words that have a starting-point in the original word but take a jump far away from it. While the first category is more universal, the second category is most subjective and personal and tied to each person's own experiences.

You may have played a group game where someone starts off with one word, then the next person says the first word they associate with it, then the next person in the group continues.

If the first person says 'apple', you will instantly see an apple, like a flash, with your inner vision. If you don't grow apples or perhaps don't even like apples, you may just give a neutral word like 'sorts' or 'tree'. If you have many memories attached to apples, you may instead say 'France' or 'Worcester' or 'custard' or 'computers' or 'New York' or 'Aunt Maggie'. The last associations do indeed have the same starting-point but they take one step further away.

■ Write (or draw) the object in the middle of a sheet of paper. Draw out lines from this point, as many as you need when you write down the words, each on one line.

■ Write **all** the words that come into your mind, even words you think are crazy or unrelated! Don't make any attempt at order, just write the words randomly as they occur to you. The point is to write down as many words as possible, to catch them in the quick flow of association flashes in your head. Don't censor and don't exclude any words! Those odd words may just be the ones that give you the best ideas later on, or that personal point of view that makes your article or speech memorable to the readers.

■ Don't worry about where you write them. If you start classifying or try to find logical connections at this stage you will lose time, a lot of good words will vanish and never be put on paper. Let your associations flow freely on to your paper. Just draw a new line for each new word and add as many as possible, no matter what they are or even if you get many words meaning the same thing. Those could be the words that give you a whole series of new words. The only rule at this stage is **abundance.**

■ Don't avoid words that involve your feelings, or very personal words. Those who try to find a structure at an early stage will lose too many words and ideas. Most of us have been trained to think logically from the very beginning of a writing process and that may hamper us the first couple of times we try this technique, but don't give up! Each skill has its own time and place in the process.

■ Look at the picture of a sailing boat. Use about five to seven minutes for the first stage in the process, ie to let out all your free associations connected to sailing.

■ If at any stage you get stuck, you only have to draw a couple of new lines somewhere from an existing word and the process will start all over again.

This is one side of the use of associations. Another and more important use in connection with the memorizing technique is the ability to make a completely new image by combining two words. Here are pairs of words that you can use to practise this ability.

example: sandal–rose

1. make a sandal that smells like a rose
2. tread among the roses with one's sandals on
3. attach roses to your sandals
4. paint a rose on the sandals
5. roses that are running around wearing sandals

As you can see, it is not necessary to keep to reality! You can create anything with your imagination as long as your images contain both words, however crazy the connection is.

---

exercise

Make at least four or five images each of the following pairs:

biscuit – car

feather – house

bed – fish

basket – water

sail – paper clip

The importance of an exercise like this is to help you 'let go'. It is important that you make use of your imagination and childishness. It is this ability to get new associations quickly that will help you to create the 'spiral' that binds together the two piles we talked about earlier.

---

rhyme and reason

If you look at page 76 again you will find the memory exercise where you were supposed to remember ten figures and words in the right combination. As you could gather from the following text you could combine the two words in an imaginary way, letting new fantastic images grow in your mind.

In the memory technique we are going to explore first, the logical part is based on words that **rhyme** with the figures. It is called the **'Number–Rhyme System'.** You can use the following rhymes for a start but if you are not happy with them you are free to change them for others, as long as they rhyme with the number.

one – bun

two – shoe

three – tree

four – floor

five – hive

six – sticks

seven – heaven

eight – gate

nine – wine

ten – hen

Learn these rhyming words together with the figures. In that way they form a unit, because when you use them, you use only the rhyming word to combine with the word you want to remember. You do that because it is easier to find an image with a bun than with the figure one, or a shoe than the figure two. There are memorizing techniques that are based on the resemblance of the figures to something else. Number one could for instance be a sword, number two could be formed into a swan, etc.

Before we try another row of ten words to remember, let's return to our piles of paper with a spiral:

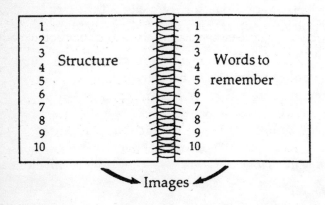

It is time to test another set of ten words. This time you use the rhyming words and combine them with the words to remember. This means that if I use number 3 and give you the word **cucumber** to remember, you pick up the rhyming word for 3 which is **tree** and make a combination of the two words in a way to meet the criteria of being: exaggerated, rude, absurd, etc.

Maybe you think of a Christmas tree with cucumbers hanging from it as decorations.

Once you get a good picture 'freeze' it and store it in your mind to pick out again when you want to recall it. If you are to succeed in recalling the word 'cucumber' again, the mental picture you create must be sharp and clear, otherwise it gets mixed up and you will lose the cucumber and find something else or nothing at all. Through trial and error you will find out what works for you.

exercise

Are you ready? You have two minutes in which to make the combinations in your mind between the rhyming words that you already have and the ten new ones.

3 - police officer	**8 - jam**
5 - house	**10 - banana**
1 - monkey	**7 - pencil**
2 - glass	**6 - nurse**
9 - car	**4 - chair**

Cover the words above and try to write down as many as you can remember:

1 _____	6 _____
2 _____	7 _____
3 _____	8 _____
4 _____	9 _____
5 _____	10 _____

Possibly you scored all ten this time, but if you did not, try again with another list of words. Results will come with practice!

These words are just nonsense words, of course, and don't worry if you can't see any immediate use for this specific technique. It is impractical in many ways – it's not easy to find rhyming words beyond ten, and you will find that the rhyming words tend to get worn out the more you use them. The reason for including this technique here is that it shows very clearly how your memory works. Soon you will get acquainted with more efficient and practical methods for daily use.

go for a memory walk

Now we are going to re-establish the contacts with the Greeks and Romans (page 75). The memorizing technique that was 'invented' by Simonides, which was described by Cicero, is called the **'Loci method'** after the Latin word *locus* which means 'locality' or 'place' = 'a method built on the use of places'.

Think of a place or an environment you are very familiar with – it could be your home, your workplace, the daily stroll to the newsagent or whatever. Choose ten objects in this place and write them down, each with a number from 1 to 10. What you have done now is to construct the logical part in this specific memorizing technique. You now have a list that corresponds to the ten rhyming words in the technique we tried previously. It is these ten places/objects you will now use to associate with the words you are to remember. Make your images ridiculous, exaggerated, vivid, moving, humorous, etc and it will work.

Before you start the exercise below, read through your list again and make sure you have clear mental pictures of all the objects in your list.

exercise

Take the words from your own list and associate them one by one and in turn with the words in the list below. Make up your own mental pictures in your head, not by writing them down.

You have two minutes to do the exercise and when you are ready, turn the book round and write down as many words as you remember.

1	soap	6	feather
2	sugar	7	letter
3	cake	8	snake
4	ruler	9	glue
5	video film	10	politician

links forming a chain

Another way of remembering things in a sequence is to use the
Link system of memory. Let's try these random 15 words:

field

ashtray

ant

axe

newspaper

chair

calculator

bread

ice

girl

tie

cow

book

shoestring

fish

This is how to do it: the first word is your starting-point, your first
link in the chain. You then associate it with the next word in a
ridiculous, exaggerated way – the sillier images you get the
better! If the images are too mundane, everyday or logical you
will not remember them.

In this case you start with the word **field** and associate that
with **ashtray.** Think of an enormous ashtray, big as a flying saucer
that has landed in a field. Now you take the next word on the list,
ant and associate that with the previous word, which was ashtray.

Imagine an ant sitting on the edge of that huge ashtray smoking a cigarette! The next association is between ant and **axe.** Maybe the ant needed an axe to cut off the ash from his cigarette? The next word is **newspaper** and as the ant didn't have a pair of scissors he used his axe instead to take cuttings from his newspaper. The next word is **chair.** Imagine a chair wrapped up with the newspapers, or a chair made of *papier mâché!* In one of the arms of the chair there was a built-in **calculator** in the form of a loaf of **bread** with buttons made of **ice.** A **girl** comes by and she is all covered in ice. She is wearing a big **tie,** it is so big that she could use it as a lasso and catch a **cow** with it. The cow was very upset because it had just started to read a good **book!** The book had been read so many times it was held together by a **shoestring,** so long that it could be used for catching **fish.**

You could make a story of it if you like, but the principle as such is very simple. Just remember to make the associations **silly, exaggerated, ridiculous, absurd, rude, moving, humorous, full of colour, bigger/smaller** or anything else so the images are unique and unusual!

Try this list of 20 new words!

exercise

Associate the following 20 words with each other like links forming a chain. You have three minutes. When you are ready, turn the book over and write down the words.

scissors – bamboo – nose – can – cat – water – file – bag – shoe – hotel – finger – oyster – silver – wallet – sheep – trumpet – nun – beach party – comb – computer

in a nutshell

■ Memory techniques are effective if they are based on **associations**.

■ The associations should be:
exaggerated in form, colour, number, size
absurd, out of the ordinary
fantastic, new combinations
unusual
unexpected
moving
ridiculous, to the point of making you laugh
full of colour, to contrast with the environment
sexual, rude
sensual, beautiful

learning maps applications

study planning

By planning your time, your studies, your shopping and so on you discover you will become more effective and purposeful in what you are doing, and you will have time for more things.

Most people are not used to planning their time or are reluctant to do so because they think it is boring, unnecessary, tedious, a hindrance to spontaneity.

But you can turn the whole thing over and say: if you don't plan your time, your studies and other things, you will easily become a victim of circumstances, ie you let others decide on how your time is spent or you are easily carried away as new impulses pop up in your head. If you lack a goal or driving force, it is more difficult for you to get an overview of your time and the work you are supposed to do. It is more difficult to separate what is important from what is unimportant; there is no time left for spontaneous activities, social calls, hobbies and other things.

The first step towards sound studying habits is taken when you start planning your time. Such planning starts by being more aware of how you spend your time now.

Use the circle below to make a pie chart of your average day. How much time do you spend sleeping, eating, working, meeting friends, hobbies, etc?

'the Swiss cheese method'

A Swiss cheese has more holes than it has cheese. The cheese might look big but as it contains so many holes the actual substance is not very big at all. If we transfer the image to studies and time planning, it means we have to make clear to ourselves what is 'hole' and what is 'substance'.

■ Always start with the **wholeness.**
   Read quickly through the text once. Use a highlighter and mark important keywords while you are reading. This first quick reading gives you a fairly good idea about the substance. You can now either leave the text to the next day or even later or take the next step. This first reading only serves the purpose of giving you the important overview, and with the keywords you have marked it will be easy to find the wholeness when you start again.
■ If you decide to leave the text for a while start the next session with a quick **revision** of the material. Just flick through and read the keywords you have marked.

- ■ **Prepare a learning map** by drawing the central point and a few of the thick branches.
- ■ Why do you read this text? What kind of information do you want? **Set a goal** for your reading. Do you do it to learn everything in it or just certain aspects? Do you read it to be able to answer questions in a test? Or do you read it to give a summary to someone else?

  You have to be well aware of the goal because that decides not only why you should read the text but also how well you should read it. You can save a lot of time by **not reading** texts you are not interested in! You discover in your first read if the text is worth reading again or not.
- ■ At this stage you have decided to read the text for some particular purpose and you have prepared a learning map. **Read** the text again, and while doing so, **add new words and pictures to the branches in your learning map.**
- ■ **Revise the material regularly.** The value of repetition is enormous. Every time you do it you can either just look through the first learning map or rewrite it, deleting words that are unnecessary. You keep only the words that are really important.

This way of working not only **saves a lot of time**, it also gives you a **quick overview** and **understanding** of what you are reading. The result is you **learn better and faster.** It also makes it easier to **revise** the material.

Now you can easily read and find the important information in any text. Once you get an idea of the wholeness and have decided on your purpose you can concentrate on the substance and leave out the 'holes'.

Remember: **You save time through planning!**

personal planning

How do you normally plan your time? Most people have a diary based on dates and times. In a diary of that kind time is superior to content. When you learn to do your planning with learning maps the content will be superior to time. That will make you see clearly what is **important to do** and not only what is to be done.

Planning with **time** as superior to content leads to an attitude that it is easier to carry out small activities instead of big, important tasks. Planning with **content** as superior to time gives you an opportunity to make priorities and get the important things done.

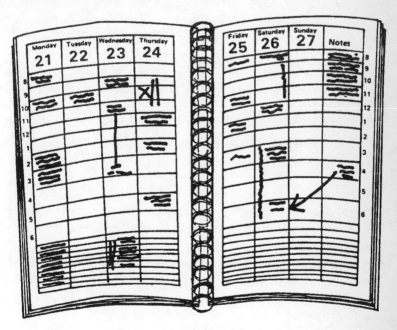

exercise

■ Use the learning map below to fill in **all** the activities, small as well as big, that you know you have to do next week.

■ Make priorities. You can use a few coloured pens and let them symbolize A–B–C or 1–2–3, whatever you like, to show different priorities.

■ Now is the time to fill in the daily plans in your diary or personal organizer. Make sure you allocate time to the tasks you have put highest priority on.

supporting a diary with learning maps

case study

'In my job as general practitioner at a hospital I face daily thick medical diaries, which take a long time to read through in order to get a proper view of a patient's medical status,' a doctor says.

'Medical diaries are added to continuously over the years with papers in A4 format, which are being filed in numerical order along with results from examinations, X-ray plates, notes of admission, ECG results, letters, etc.

'This means it is normally very difficult to get an overview of patients with a long history of various illnesses and visits to clinics.

'I use mind maps instead of a traditional diary. It takes about 10 to 15 minutes to make one but I gain those minutes every time I have to revise a patient's records when a person comes to visit me.'

Below is an example of one of those learning maps:

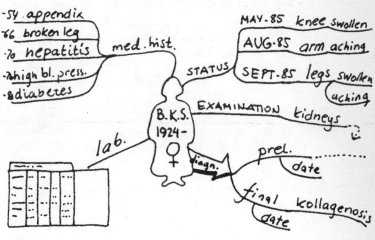

Medical history

meetings

Most of us will attend several kinds of meetings in our lives – union meetings, project meetings, board meetings, club meetings and many others. At those meetings there is normally an agenda and there is a secretary who eventually writes the minutes. Being the secretary at a meeting is not a job people run for. It also happens now and then that you get boring minutes to read after a meeting and you even wonder what happened because of the poor information contained in the minutes.

Many secretaries see it as their main task to write down as much as possible from the meeting. This necessarily means they can't take an active part in the discussion at the meeting. If the secretary takes his or her notes in the form of a learning map it is easier to keep up with the discussion as he or she is concentrating on finding a few important keywords.

This is what the secretary's notes look like after a meeting. A learning map does not replace ordinary minutes – it is a piece of paper with personal notes and it is the only help the secretary needs to write the minutes.

A learning map is always personal!

budgets

When people say they don't understand a budget it is usually because they only see a lot of figures on a complicated form. Really, a budget is **wishes expressed in the form of figures.**

A budget is supposed to express what you want to do over a certain period, mostly one year. It also expresses how much faith you have in what you are doing, how much you expect to sell or whatever your business is.

In traditional budgets figures are the most important part, and then the contents of the business. Using a learning map for budgeting forces you to do it the other way round, maybe the way it should be done. You start by writing down what you would like to accomplish and then allocate sufficient funds to implement it.

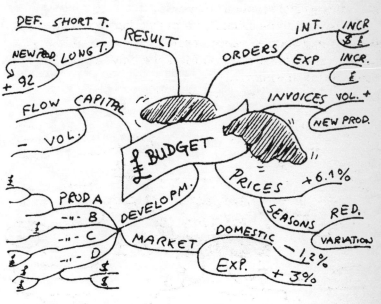

learning maps in business and financial analysis

case study

'When we make an initial contact with a client we make a thorough analysis of that company. Before I do the analysis, I write down a few keywords for that specific company,' says a consultant.

'My starting-point for the analysis is the factors that describe the company. They make me see where I can step in and help that company to make its activities more effective. The most important thing is to get an overview. What is the company like today and how do they organize their administrative and operational routines? What is done manually and what is done by machines and computers? What are the volumes? Where are the problems?

'Looking at a factor such as **personal effectiveness** we go through jobs that involve finance, marketing, planning, correspondence, invoicing, calculations, word processing, etc.

'To use it is a matter of "qualifying" the client. By "qualify" we mean what we want to know whether our solutions will suit this specific client. Our solutions are at present linked to personal computers as the use of a PC will raise the level of personal effectiveness in the companies we are working with.

'Before I attended one of Ingemar's seminars and got the idea to use learning maps for analyses, I had a large number of questionnaires and forms, which were complicated to adapt to each client. They also took a very long time to fill in. With a mind map I get an overview very quickly, I can discover the weak spots and both the client and I save time.

'When you work with analyses you must get overview and wholeness as a result, and learning mapping is a better and quicker way to do it.'

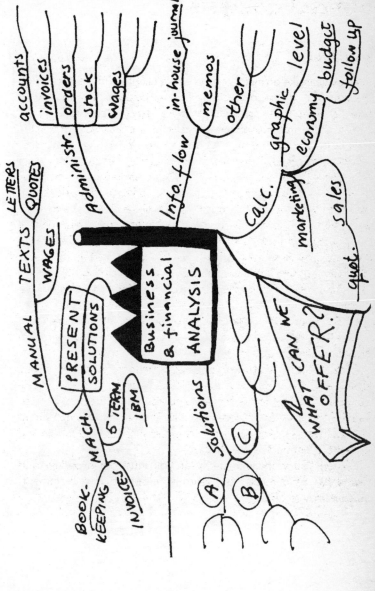

Business and financial analysis

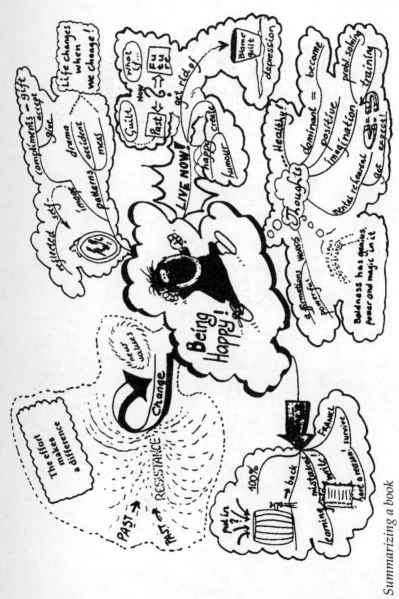

Summarizing a book

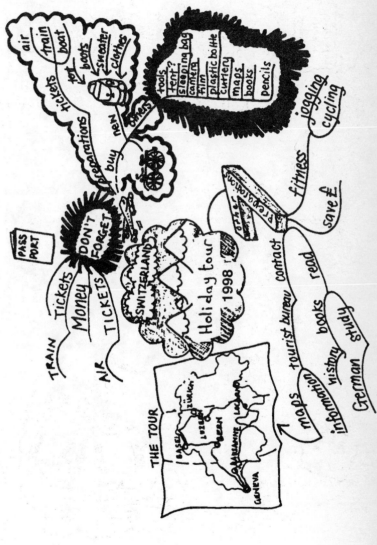

Planning a holiday

learning maps: summary

select bibliography

Adams, J L (1986) *The Care and Feeding of Ideas – A Guide to Encouraging Creativity*, Penguin, London

Albrecht, K (1980) *Brain Power: Learn to Improve Your Thinking Skills*, Prentice-Hall, Englewood Cliffs, NJ

Bono, E de (1977) *Lateral Thinking*, Penguin, London

Buzan, T (1984) *Use Your Head*, Ariel Books / BBC Books, London

Buzan, T (1986) *Use Your Memory*, BBC Books, London

Buzan, T (1993) *The Mind Map Book,* BBC Books, London

Edwards, B (1982) *Drawing on the Right Side of the Brain*, Fontana, London

Hyerle, D (1996) *Visual Tools for Constructing Knowledge*, Association for Supervision and Curriculum Development, Alexandria, VA

Hyerle, D (2000) *A Field Guide to Using Visual Tools*, Association for Supervision and Curriculum Development, Alexandria, VA

Lorayne, H (1986) *How to Develop a Super-Power Memory*, Thorsons, London

Margulies, N (1991) *Mapping Inner Space: Learning and teaching mind mapping*, Zephyr Press, Tucson, AZ

Ornstein, R, and Thompson, R F (1985) *The Amazing Brain*, Chatto & Windus, London

Redway, K (1988) *Rapid Reading*, Pan, London

Rico, G L (1983) *Writing the Natural way*, J P Tarcher, Los Angeles, CA

Rose, C (1984) *Accelerated Learning*, Accelerated Learning Systems, Minneapolis, MA

Russell, P (1980) *The Brain Book; Know Your Own Mind and How to Use It*, Routledge & Kegan Paul, London

Schacter, D (1996) *In Search of Memory*, HarperCollins, London

Shone, R (1984) *Creative Visualization*, Thorsons, London

Yates, F A (1984) *The Art of Memory*, Ark

puzzle solution

Puzzle on page 18

Can you see the cat?

memory exercise

Here are the 30 words for the memory test described on pages 71–72. You have 10 minutes to find three cues to each of the following words. Write them down on a note pad. Read through and follow the instructions on page 72.

bridge	bottle
saddle	tomato
Christmas shopping	pie
burglar alarm	elevator
bag	silver
smith	sponge
settee	stamp
typewriter	monkey
mouse	ruler
envelope	lake
keys	dirt
tape	copier
Columbus	fantasy
bicycle	asparagus
apricot	yellow